Habitats

All About
Forests

by Christina Mia Gardeski

raintree
a Capstone company — publishers for children

Raintree is an imprint of Capstone Global Library Limited, a company incorporated in England and Wales having its registered office at 264 Banbury Road, Oxford, OX2 7DY – Registered company number: 6695582

www.raintree.co.uk
myorders@raintree.co.uk

Edited by Nick Healy
Designed by Juliette Peters
Picture research by Wanda Winch
Production by Steve Walker
Originated by Capstone Global Library Limited
Printed and bound in China

ISBN 978-1-4747-4721-9
21 20 19 18 17
10 9 8 7 6 5 4 3 2 1

British Library Cataloguing-in-Publication Data
A full catalogue record for this book is available from the British Library

Acknowledgements
We would like to thank the following for permission to reproduce photographs: Dreamstime: Bchancha, 21, Betty4240, 15, Lucidwaters, 11; Shutterstock: David Boutin, 7, Erik Mandre, 1, Ermakov Alexander, 17, Grigoriy Pil, 9, Helena-art, tree design, Henrik Larsson, 19, Jeff Feverston, cover, jurra8, 13, Sara van Netten, 5

Every effort has been made to contact copyright holders of material reproduced in this book. Any omissions will be rectified in subsequent printings if notice is given to the publisher.

Contents

What is a forest?

A forest is a land of trees.

The trees grow close together.

Some trees have leaves.

The leaves change colour in autumn.

They fall off by winter.

Other trees have needles.

They stay green all year.

In the treetops

The trees grow tall.

Branches cover the forest.

It is a shady habitat.

11

Many animals live here.

Owls spy on mice.

Squirrels pick acorns.

owl

On the ground

Some trees fall.

Skunks live in the old logs.

Snakes hide under logs.

skunks

Mushrooms grow on the logs.

Deer eat the mushrooms.

Ants eat the old wood.

The wood turns into soil.

Growing Up

Animals carry seeds.

Seeds blow in the wind.

Seeds fall in the soil.

The forest grows.

Glossary

acorn seed of an oak tree

forest land filled with trees that grow close together

habitat home of a plant or animal

leaf part of a plant that grows from the stem

log big tree trunk that has been cut down or has fallen to the ground

mushroom fungus with a stem and flat cap

needle leaf of an evergreen tree

soil dirt in which plants can grow

treetop top of a tree

Read more

Forest Life and Woodland Creatures (Practical Facts), DK (DK Children, 2017)

i-SPY Trees: What Can You Spot? (Collins Michelin i-SPY Guides), i-SPY (Collins, 2016)

Woodland Creatures (Usborne Young Beginners), Emily Bone (Usborne, 2017)

Websites

www.forestry.gov.uk/visit

http://scotland.forestry.gov.uk/

www.woodlandtrust.org.uk/naturedetectives/

Index